OUR PLACES OF WORSHIP

Islam

Honor Head

WAYLAND

First published in 2009
by Wayland

Copyright © Wayland 2009

Wayland
338 Euston Road
London NW1 3BH

Wayland Australia
Level 17/207 Kent Street
Sydney NSW 2000

Commissioning editor: Jennifer Sanderson
Editor: Jean Coppendale
Designer: Paul Manning
Consultant: Dr Fatma Amer, Senior Lecturer
   in Islamic Education

British Library Cataloguing in Publication Data
Head, Honor.
Islam. — (Our places of worship)
1. Mosques—Juvenile literature.
2. Islam—Customs and practices
Juvenile literature.
I. Title II. Series
297.3'51-dc22

ISBN 978 0 7502 4925 6

Picture credits

l = left r = right t = top b = bottom
Cover, 4, 5, 7, 8, 11, 16t, 20, 21, 22t, 23 Discovery Media/Our Places of Worship;
6 Valery Shanin/Shutterstock; 9t/b Distinctive Images/Shutterstock; 10 Roland
Liptak/Alamy; 12 Andrew Fox/Alamy; 13 Jeremy King/ArkReligion.com; 14 Ed
Kashi/Corbis; 15 Trip/ArkReligion.com; 16 Athar Akram/ArkReligion.com/Alamy;
17 Louise Batalla Duran/Alamy; 18 Kazuyoshi Nomachi/
Corbis; 19 Paul Cowan/Shutterstock; 24 Aamir Qureshi/
Getty; 25 Trip/ArkReligion.com; 26 ArkReligion.com/
Alamy; 27 ayazad/Shutterstock; 28 Athar Akram/
ArkReligion.com; 29 ayazad/Shutterstock

Printed in China

Wayland is a division of Hachette Children's
Books, an Hachette UK company.
www.hachette.co.uk

This book can be used in conjunction with the interactive CD-Rom, *Our Places of Worship*. To do this, look for ⊙ and the file path. For example, material on mosques can be found on ⊙ Islam/Mosques/Types of mosques. From the main menu of the CD, click on 'Islam', then 'Mosques' and then 'Types of mosques'.

To see a sample from the CD-Rom, log on to www.waylandbooks.co.uk.

Our Places of Worship
Single user licence: ISBN 978 0 7502 5303 1
School library service licence: ISBN 978 0 7502 5532 5
Site user licence ISBN 978 0 7502 5533 2

Note: When Muslims use the name of the Prophet Muhammad they usually follow it with the blessing 'Peace be upon him'. This is shown in the text here as '(pbuh)'.

Contents

Words appearing in **bold**, like this, can be found in the glossary on page 30.

What is a mosque?

A mosque, or masjid, is where Muslims go to worship and study the scriptures. Muslims follow a religion called Islam and believe in one God, called Allah. Muslims can visit a mosque whenever they wish but they have a duty to pray five times a day at certain times. When Muslims pray, they must face in the direction of the city of **Makkah** in Saudi Arabia, where the holy **Ka'ba** is situated.

◀ The Shah Jahan mosque in Woking, Surrey, is the oldest Muslim place of worship in England.

Domes and minarets

Mosques can be very beautiful, **ornate** buildings or simple spaces with **prayer mats**. A mosque usually has a large dome and tall towers called minarets.

A person called a mu'adhin gives the Adhan (call to prayer) from the top of a minaret five times a day. In some countries, such as England, the Adhan is usually made from inside the mosque.

▼ This mosque is in Luton, England. It has a gold-coloured dome and a tall minaret.

minaret

dome

MAKKAH

Makkah is a city in Saudi Arabia. It is where Islam began and is the most holy place for Muslims. Millions of Muslims visit Makkah every year on a special **pilgrimage** to visit the Ka'ba (see page 27).

Welcome to the mosque

Most Muslims go to the mosque on Fridays for special prayers (see page 17). Men and boys worship separately from the women and girls. Sometimes the women's area is a balcony overlooking the **prayer hall**. In the prayer hall is a mihrab, or arch, in one of the walls. The mihrab is often highly decorated and designed to look like a doorway or a passage to Makkah.

▼ Worshippers face the mihrab when they pray so they know that they are facing towards Makkah and the Ka'ba.

mihrab

Getting ready for prayer

Muslims take off their shoes when they enter the mosque. This shows respect and helps to keep the prayer hall clean. Before they go into the prayer hall, Muslims wash in a special way called wudu. First they wash their hands, then mouth and nose, then face, then arms up to their elbows, and then their feet. Finally, they cover their head to show respect to Allah.

▲ Muslims remove their shoes inside the mosque.

◀ Muslims wash in a special way called wudu before going into the prayer hall.
This is always done in the same order:
1. face
2. arms
3. feet

● Islam/Worship/Friday Prayers

In the prayer hall

In the prayer hall, an **imam** (see pages 10-11) leads the prayers and gives a sermon called the khutba. In his sermon, the imam may explain a passage from the **Qur'an,** the Muslim holy book (see pages 20-21), or talk about the life of the **Prophet Muhammad** (pbuh) (see pages 18-19). The imam may also talk about how Muslims can be true to their beliefs in their daily lives.

▼ There are no tables or chairs in the prayer hall. Worshippers sit on prayer mats on the floor.

Saying prayers

After the imam's sermon, salah, or prayers, begin. Muslims pray with their whole bodies. They perform a series of movements called rak'a. Some of the movements are standing to attention with the hands across the body, then bowing, and then kneeling and touching the ground with the forehead as a sign of respect to Allah. Finally, they turn their head to the left and to the right to show that prayer has ended. After prayers, most Muslims go back to work. Others stay at the mosque to meet friends and to chat.

▶ Bowing (right) and touching their forehead to the ground (below) is what Muslims do when they pray.

WHAT DO YOU THINK?

Why is it important to pray every day?

Why do you think Muslims do wudu before they pray?

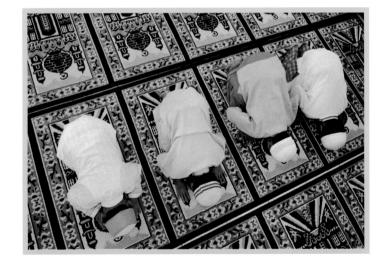

The imam

An imam is the leader of a local Muslim community. He is chosen by the people who go to the mosque where he leads prayers and other special services. The imam must know the Qur'an by memory and know all about the history of Islam, Islamic law and the life of the Prophet Muhammad (pbuh).

▼ Part of the job of the imam is to perform special ceremonies, such as weddings.

imam

INTERVIEW WITH AN IMAM

This Muslim boy, Hanzala, asks the imam how he decides what to talk about in the sermon.

This is what the imam says:

"Every month there are certain events and topics that I talk about. In the month of **Rabi al-Awwal**, I speak about the birth of the Prophet Muhammad (pbuh). During the month of **Ramadan** (see page 14), I will speak about **fasting**. But I also look at any issues that concern the Muslim community: something that is on the news or that is happening locally."

What Muslims believe

Muslims have five main duties, called the Five Pillars of Islam, which they must follow throughout their lives.

Shahadah

The first pillar is called the shahadah, and it is the most important rule for Muslims to follow. This is that there is no other God except Allah and that the Prophet Muhammad (pbuh) is Allah's messenger (see pages 18-19). Muslims repeat this belief each morning when they wake up, before they go to sleep, and before every prayer.

▼ Young Muslims go to a madrasah, a special school held in the mosque. At the madrasah they learn about Islamic beliefs.

◉ Islam/Mosques/Inside the Mosque/Madrasahs

◀ Wherever they are, Muslims stop what they are doing at the same time every day to pray. They do not have to be in a mosque.

Prayer

The second of the five pillars is salah, or prayer. Muslims consider that prayer is the most important thing they do and they must pray five times a day. Whatever they are doing, or wherever they are, Muslims must stop and pray at the set times (see pages 16-17).

Giving to the poor

The third pillar is called zakah. This is giving money to the poor and needy. All Muslims believe they should give money to the poor each year. The money is used for many things. It could be used to build a hospital or mosque, or to feed and clothe a family.

WHAT DO YOU THINK?

Why do you think prayer is an important part of most religions?

Why do you think Muslims pray at the same time each day, five times a day?

Fasting

The fourth pillar, sawm, is to fast for the month of Ramadan every year. For 30 days, most Muslims should not eat or drink anything during the daytime. When they fast, Muslims think about the teachings of Allah and about people who do not have enough food to eat. They read the Qur'an more often, at home and in the mosque.

A family meal

After sunset, people who are fasting have a sip of water and some dates to end the fast for that day. Then they have a meal with the family. The fast begins again the next morning at sunrise.

WHO FASTS AT RAMADAN?

All Muslims should fast. Children first start to fast when they are eight years old, but only for a few days. They do not do a proper fast until they are about 12 or 13 years old. The elderly, pregnant women and people who are ill, do not have to fast.

▼ During Ramadan, after evening prayers at the end of each day, families share a meal.

Pilgrimage

The fifth pillar is to make a pilgrimage, called **Hajj**, to the city of Makkah in Saudi Arabia. Every Muslim who can, must make this journey at least once (see pages 26-27). Millions of Muslims from around the world make the Hajj every year.

(see pages 26-27)

▼ These Muslims on Hajj are boarding their aeroplane to Saudi Arabia.

WHAT DO YOU THINK?

Why is it important that Muslims follow all the Five Pillars?

Why do you think fasting is part of the Muslim religion?

Muslims at prayer

Muslims pray five times a day. They pray once in the morning, three times during the day, and then finally in the evening. At these times Muslims stop what they are doing, take off their shoes and pray. Muslims will try to put down a prayer mat, or even a sheet of newspaper to kneel on, so that they are not praying on the dirty ground.

▲ A clock on the wall in the mosque shows the times that Muslims have to pray each day.

▲ In some countries the mosque is not big enough for all the worshippers to pray inside, so many pray outside the mosque.

Friday prayers

Muslims also pray at home and often have a special room, or part of a room, set aside for prayer. They have a sign on the wall to show them the direction of the Ka'bah in Makkah. The most important prayers of the week are said on Friday at midday, and most Muslims try to go to a mosque to pray at this time.

Women and prayer

Muslim men and women both pray in the mosque, but women sit in a private area or at the back of the main prayer hall. Most women prefer to pray at home, especially if they have a family to look after, but some go to the mosque for Friday prayers.

WHAT DO YOU THINK?

Why do you think praying in a mosque is different from praying at home?

◀ In the mosque there are separate areas where women pray.

The Prophet Muhammad (pbuh)

Muhammad (pbuh) was born in the city of Makkah. His parents died when he was young and he was brought up by his grandparents. Muhammad's (pbuh) family was poor and he did not learn to read or write. When he was old enough, he went to work with his uncle who was a trader. At this time, many people in Makkah drank a lot of alcohol, fought each other in the streets, and worshipped statues.

▼ Today, many large, modern buildings fill the city of Makkah in Saudi Arabia, the birthplace of the Prophet Muhammad (pbuh).

The Angel Jibrael

Muhammad (pbuh) spent a lot of time thinking about God. One night, when he was praying in a cave, Muhammad (pbuh) had a **vision.** In the vision, the Angel Jibrael came to visit him and told him that he would be God's messenger. He was to tell the people that there was only one God, called Allah. Muhammad (pbuh) also had to explain how God wanted all people to live and to behave.

WHAT DO YOU THINK?

Why do you think Allah chose Muhammad (pbuh) to be his messenger?

Why do you think it is important that Muslims follow the words of Allah?

God's messenger

Over the years, Muhammad (pbuh) was given lots of different messages from Allah. Later, these were put together in the Qur'an. Muhammad (pbuh) became known as the Prophet and Messenger of God.

▲ Muslim pilgrims visit the cave of Hira near Makkah, where Muhammad (pbuh) received messages from the Angel Jibrael.

The Qur'an

The Qur'an is the Muslim holy book. It gives Muslims guidance on how they should live and behave each day, how they should treat each other and how they should worship Allah. It also has stories about the history of Islam. Muslims believe that the words of the Qur'an come from Allah through the Angel Jibrael.

▼ The Qur'an tells Muslims how to lead good lives and obey Allah's laws.

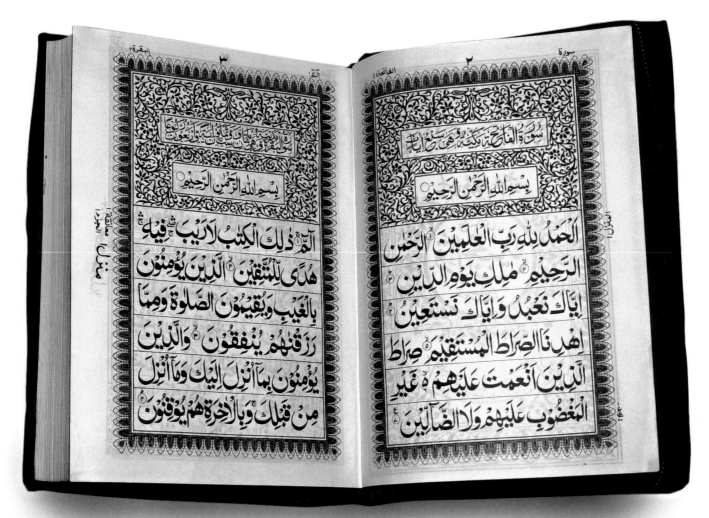

⊙ Islam/Worship/Reading the Qur'an

Learning Arabic

The Qur'an was written in **Arabic** and it is always read in Arabic. However, Muslims who do not speak Arabic may have a copy in their own language. After school, or at weekends, many Muslim children go to the mosque to learn Arabic so that they can read and study the Qur'an.

▼ These children are learning to read the Qur'an at their mosque. They put the holy book on a special stand to keep it clean.

CARE FOR THE QUR'AN

The Qur'an is always treated with great care and respect. At home, when it is not in use, it is kept on a high shelf to keep it safe and to make sure it is not damaged.

Signs and symbols

There are many important Islamic signs and symbols. One is the crescent moon and star used to decorate mosques and flags. Islam began in a part of the world where it is very hot during the day, so people often travelled at night when it was cooler. They were guided by the positions of the stars and the light from the moon, which they believe were all created by Allah.

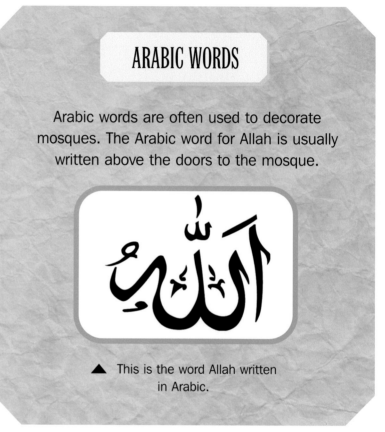

ARABIC WORDS

Arabic words are often used to decorate mosques. The Arabic word for Allah is usually written above the doors to the mosque.

▲ This is the word Allah written in Arabic.

▶ The flag of Pakistan shows the symbol of the crescent moon and star.

⊙ Islam/Signs, Symbols and Religious Objects

Prayer beads

Sets of prayer beads called tasbih hang in every mosque. Each set has three lots of 33 beads. Each bead stands for a name for Allah, such as the Wise, the Good, and the Merciful. Worshippers touch a bead and say the name, which helps them to think about Allah and to feel close to him.

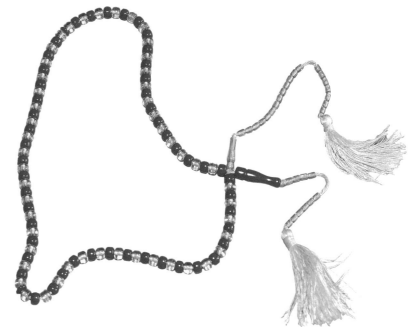

▲ Most worshippers have their own tasbih. Each bead stands for one of the 99 names for Allah.

Head coverings

Most Muslims cover their head in the mosque as a sign of respect for Allah. Men often wear a small prayer cap and many Muslim women wear a hijab to cover their head and shoulders. Muslims believe that Allah has asked them to do this so that they are not judged on how they look, but on the person they are.

◀ Muslim women wear a hijab that covers all their hair. They wear this when they go out and in the mosque.

⊙ Islam/Signs, Symbols and Religious Objects

Islamic festivals

Ramadan is the most important time of year for Muslims. It celebrates the month when Allah gave the first words of the Qur'an to the Prophet Muhammad (pbuh). At Ramadan, Muslims fast for a month and give thanks for all the good things they have. Eid ul-Fitr is the festival that marks the end of Ramadan and fasting. Muslims visit the mosque to thank Allah for giving them the strength to fast.

▼ These Muslim worshippers are celebrating the festival of Eid ul-Fitr at the end of Ramadan.

Eid ul-Adha

Another important festival is Eid ul-Adha. At this festival, Muslims remember the story of Ibrahim and his son, Ismail. Allah asked Ibrahim to **sacrifice** his only son as a test to show his love for Allah. Just as Ibrahim was about to do this, Allah stopped him. Eid ul-Adha takes place on the last day of the Hajj (see pages 26-27). On this day, Muslims go to the mosque for special prayers.

Birthday of the Prophet

Many Muslims celebrate Mawlid al-Nabi, the birthday of the Prophet Muhammad (pbuh). In some Muslim countries, street parades are held and mosques and homes are decorated. The imam might give a special talk about Muhammad (pbuh), what he did, and how Muslims can follow his example.

(see pages 26-27)

WHAT DO YOU THINK?

Why do you think religious festivals are important?

What do you think is the best way to celebrate a religious festival?

▶ In Bangladesh, Muslims celebrate Mawlid al-Nabi – the Day of the Prophet – with a big street parade.

Holy places

One of the holiest places in the world for Muslims is the city of Makkah. The Hajj, or pilgrimage to Makkah, is one of the Five Pillars of Islam (see page 15). The Hajj is very important for Muslims and is done towards the end of the year. Men who make the Hajj wear special clothes called ihram. These are simple cotton sheets, which are usually white. Wearing the ihram shows that no matter how rich or poor they are, everyone is the same before Allah.

▲ Muslims on Hajj can buy simple meals from roadside stalls.

The Ka'ba

Muslims go to Makkah to see the Ka'ba, which means 'cube'. This is a small stone building that Muslims believe was built by Ibrahim and his son, Ismail, to worship Allah. The Ka'ba is the holiest building for Muslim pilgrims. It is in the courtyard of the **Great Mosque**.

▼ Muslims believe the Ka'ba was the first place built for the worship of Allah.

the Ka'ba is covered by a black cloth made of silk and cotton

The Well of Zamzam

In the courtyard of the Great Mosque is the Well of Zamzam. Muslims believe this well was shown to the Prophet Ibrahim's wife by the Angel Jibrael when she was desperately searching for water. Many pilgrims drink from the well, and some take water from the well home for friends and family to drink.

◀ Pilgrims in Makkah fill plastic bottles with holy water from the Well of Zamzam to take home.

City of Madinah

Muhammad (pbuh) left Makkah because the people there continued to fight and worship statues and would not believe in Allah. The Prophet travelled to Madinah where he told people about Allah and how Allah wanted them to live. The people in Madinah listened, they followed the laws Muhammad (pbuh) gave them and became the first Muslims.

Death of Muhammad (pbuh)

Later, the people of Makkah also became Muslims. However, Muhammad (pbuh) stayed in Madinah where he died. His tomb lies in the Mosque of the Prophet Muhammad (pbuh). This mosque is the second holiest place in the world for Muslims. They visit the mosque to show their respect and love for Muhammad (pbuh).

▼ The Mosque of the Prophet in Madinah stands on the place where Muhammad (pbuh) once built his own, much smaller, mosque.

Glossary

Arabic the language used by Muslims for anything to do with their religion. The Qur'an is written in Arabic and Muslims pray in Arabic

fasting to go without food and drink for a time

Great Mosque the first place to be built for the worship of Allah. The Ka'ba is situated there

Hajj the journey to the Great Mosque in Makkah to visit the Ka'ba. Hajj happens every year in December. Most Muslims go on Hajj at least once in their lives

imam The person who leads the prayers in a mosque

Ka'ba a cube-shaped building that is in the courtyard of the Great Mosque in Makkah, Saudi Arabia. The Ka'ba is the most important place of worship for Muslims. All Muslims face the direction of the Ka'ba whenever they pray

Makkah a holy city for Muslims in Saudi Arabia

ornate something that has lots of decoration

pilgrimage a journey to an important holy place

pilgrims people who go on a pilgrimage

prayer hall a room inside the mosque where Muslims pray

prayer mats mats laid on the floor that worshippers use when they are praying

Prophet Muhammad (pbuh) a great messenger who passed on Allah's words to the people

Qur'an the Muslim holy book

Rabi al-Awwal the third month in the Islamic calendar and the month of Muhammad's (pbuh) birth

Ramadan the month when all Muslims fast

sacrifice to kill something and offer it as a gift to Allah

vision when a person sees someone who is dead or something that is not real

Quizzes

Try these quizzes to see how much you remember about Islam.

Are these facts true or false?

1. Muslims have to pray eight times a day.

2. The Muslim holy book is called the Qur'an.

3. The Prophet Muhammad (pbuh) was a messenger from Allah.

4. The crescent moon and star is a special symbol for Muslims.

5. During Ramadan, Muslims fast for three days.

Put the pictures below in the correct order to show what Muslims do before they enter the prayer hall in a mosque.

B

D

A

C

Answers are on the next page.

Index

Answers

1 False, they must pray five times a day.
2 True
3 True
4 True
5 False, they fast for a month.

Put the pictures in the correct order: D; B; A; C.

OUR PLACES OF WORSHIP

Contents of titles in the series:

WAYLAND